WHAT'S WITH THE LONG NAPS, BEARS?

Learning About Hibernation with

THE GARBAGE GANG

by Thomas Kingsley Troupe

illustrated by Derek Toye

PICTURE WINDOW BOOKS
a capstone imprint

MEET THE GARBAGE GANG:

SAM HAMMWICH

Sam is a once-delicious sandwich that has a bit of lettuce and tomato. He is usually crabby and a bit of a loudmouth.

GORDY

Gordy is a small rhino who wears an eyepatch even though he doesn't need one. He lives in the city dump. His friends don't visit him in the smelly dump, so Gordy created his own friends—the Garbage Gang!

SOGGY

Soggy is a stuffed bear from a carnival game. She fell into a puddle of dumpster juice and has never been the same.

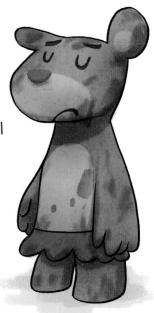

RICK

Rick is a brick. He is terrified of bugs, especially bees, which is odd ... since he's a brick.

CANN-DEE

Cann-Dee is a robot made of aluminum cans. She can pull random facts out of thin air.

MR. FRIGID

Mr. Frigid is a huge refrigerator that sprouted arms and legs. He doesn't say much, but he's super strong.

You picked the smelliest spot in town!

Need some help? I'm pretty good at building stuff.

That would be great. I just need sticks, leaves, and twigs to build a nest.

Whoa! A nest? Are you a bear or a bird?

6

Ah, you're going to hibernate! I always wondered: What's up with the long naps, bears?

Maybe they stay up too late, Gordy.

No, that's not it.

Bears ... tired.

Well, not exactly.

Are bears just lazy?

All great guesses, but no.

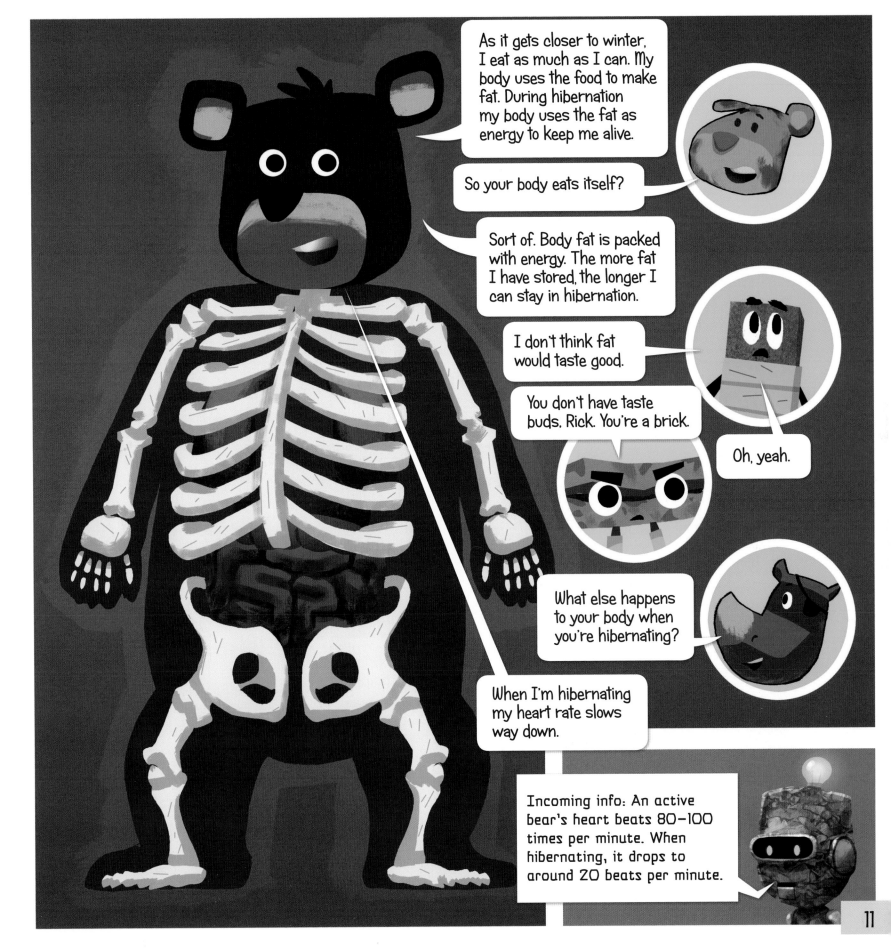

As it gets closer to winter, I eat as much as I can. My body uses the food to make fat. During hibernation my body uses the fat as energy to keep me alive.

So your body eats itself?

Sort of. Body fat is packed with energy. The more fat I have stored, the longer I can stay in hibernation.

I don't think fat would taste good.

You don't have taste buds, Rick. You're a brick.

Oh, yeah.

What else happens to your body when you're hibernating?

When I'm hibernating my heart rate slows way down.

Incoming info: An active bear's heart beats 80–100 times per minute. When hibernating, it drops to around 20 beats per minute.

11

13

So, do all animals hibernate? I'm pretty sure rhinos don't.

Mammals are the only animals that truly hibernate. But other animals have rest periods like hibernation.

Like which ones, Otto?

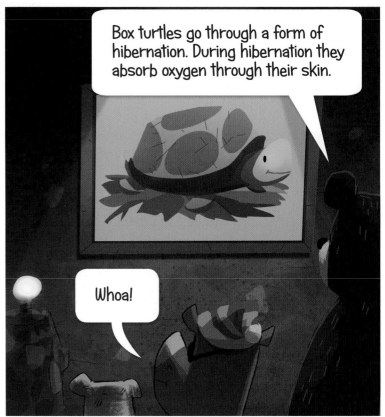

Box turtles go through a form of hibernation. During hibernation they absorb oxygen through their skin.

Whoa!

A wood frog in a cold climate hibernates. Its hibernation state is called torpor. During torpor a wood frog stops breathing, and its body partially freezes. In spring the frog thaws out again.

Frogs are OK. It's bugs I don't like.

Speaking of bugs, some bumblebees hibernate too. A queen bumblebee survives winter by hibernating underground. The other bumblebees all die before winter arrives.

That's crazy. The queen is the sole survivor, eh?

Oh, geez.

Pretty much. In spring she comes out, finds a good spot to build a nest, and creates a new army of bees.

And let's not forget about bats. Some bats can hibernate for more than six months. Some hibernating bats take just one breath every two hours.

I'm out of breath just thinking about it.

Random fact nugget downloaded: During hibernation a bat's heart rate drops from 300–400 beats per minute to as low as 10.

Estimate?

Estivate.

Salivate?

Estivate. Estivation is like hibernation in hot weather.

Why do they estivate?

Animals, like this spadefoot toad, estivate when it's too hot for them to survive. During estivation, their bodies preserve water.

Which animals estivate?

Mostly cold-blooded amphibians and reptiles. They usually bury themselves underground to keep from drying out in the heat.

Data Drop #453.1: Some animals, such as squirrels, are able to both hibernate AND estivate.

You look ready to shut down, Otto. Let's get you into your den.

17

Glossary

amphibian—an animal that lives in the water when it is young and on land as an adult; some amphibians, such as frogs, can live both in water and on land as adults

climate—average weather of a place throughout the year

estivate—to spend time in a deep sleep during dry or hot periods

habitat—the natural place and conditions in which a plant or animal lives

hibernate—to spend winter in a deep sleep; animals hibernate to survive low temperatures and lack of food

migrate—to move from one place to another

reptile—a cold-blooded animal that breathes air and has a backbone; most reptiles have scales

torpor—a state of physical or mental inactivity

You're looking up words? That's one smart move, kid!

Read More

De la Bédoyère, Camilla. *Bears*. 100 Things You Should Know About. Broomall, Penn.: Mason Crest Publishers, 2009.

Mebane, Jeanie. *Animal Hibernation*. Learn About Animal Behavior. North Mankato, Minn.: Capstone Press, 2013.

Nelson, Robin. *Hibernation*. Discovering Nature's Cycles. Minneapolis: Lerner, 2011.

Incoming data suggests that books don't stink.

Critical Thinking Using the Common Core

1. What is hibernation and why do animals do it? Name three animals that hibernate. (Key Ideas and Details)

2. Humans don't hibernate, but how do we get ready for cold weather? (Integration of Knowedge and Ideas)

Index

bats, 15
body fat, 11
breathing, 12, 14, 15
bumblebees, 15
estivation, 16–17
food, 8–9, 11
heart rate, 11, 15
mammals, 14

migration, 19, 20–21
peeing and pooping, 12
torpor, 14
winter, 8–9, 20
wood frogs, 14

Internet Sites

FactHound offers a safe, fun way to find Internet sites related to this book. All of the sites on FactHound have been researched by our staff.

Here's all you do:

Visit *www.facthound.com*

Type in this code: 9781479570560

Super-cool stuff! Check out projects, games and lots more at **www.capstonekids.com**

Thanks to our adviser for his expertise, research, and advice:
Christopher T. Ruhland, PhD
Professor of Biological Sciences
Department of Biology
Minnesota State University, Mankato

Editor: Shelly Lyons
Designer: Aruna Rangarajan
Creative Director: Nathan Gassman
Production Specialist: Morgan Walters

The illustrations in this book were created digitally
Picture Window Books are published by Capstone,
1710 Roe Crest Drive, North Mankato, Minnesota 56003
www.capstonepub.com

Library of Congress Cataloging-in-Publication Data
Troupe, Thomas Kingsley, author.
What's with the long naps, bears? : learning about hibernation with the Garbage Gang / by Thomas Kingsley Troupe.
pages cm. — (Picture Window books. The Garbage Gang's super science questions)
Summary: "Humorous text and characters help teach kids about hibernation"— Provided by publisher.
Audience: Ages 5-7
Audience: K to grade 3
Includes bibliographical references and index.
ISBN 978-1-4795-7056-0 (library binding)
ISBN 978-1-4795-7066-9 (eBook PDF)
1. Bears—Hibernation—Juvenile literature. 2. Hibernation—Juvenile literature. I. Title. II. Title: What is with the long naps, bears?
QL737.C27T76 2016
599.78'1565—dc23   2014049608

Printed in the United States of America in North Mankato, Minnesota.
032015   008823CGF15

Look for all the books in the series:

ARE BOWLING BALLS BULLIES? Learning About Forces and Motion with **THE GARBAGE GANG**

DO ANTS GET LOST? Learning About Animal Communication with **THE GARBAGE GANG**

DO BEES POOP? Learning About Living and Nonliving Things with **THE GARBAGE GANG**

DO PLANTS HAVE HEADS? Learning About Plant Parts with **THE GARBAGE GANG**

WHAT'S WITH THE LONG NAPS, BEARS? Learning About Hibernation with **THE GARBAGE GANG**

WHY DO DEAD FISH FLOAT? Learning About Matter with **THE GARBAGE GANG**

WHY DOES MY BODY MAKE BUBBLES? Learning About the Digestive System with **THE GARBAGE GANG**

YOU CALL THAT A NOSE? Learning About Human Senses with **THE GARBAGE GANG**

More books! Are you kidding me? This is the best news since sliced bread!

Seriously?